# THE 10

# Mightiest Mountains

## Nigel Samuel

Series Editor
**Jeffrey D. Wilhelm**

Much thought, debate, and research went into choosing and ranking the 10 items in each book in this series. We realize that everyone has his or her own opinion of what is most significant, revolutionary, amazing, deadly, and so on. As you read, you may agree with our choices, or you may be surprised — and that's the way it should be!

**Franklin Watts**
an imprint of
**SCHOLASTIC**
www.scholastic.com/librarypublishing

A Rubicon book published in association with Scholastic Inc.

Ru'bicon © 2008 Rubicon Publishing Inc.
**www.rubiconpublishing.com**

 is a trademark of The 10 Books

Associate Publishers: Kim Koh, Miriam Bardswich
Project Editor: Amy Land
Editoral Assistant: Nikki Yeh
Creative Director: Jennifer Drew
Project Manager/Designer: Jeanette MacLean
Graphic Designer: Katherine Park

The publisher gratefully acknowledges the following for permission to reprint copyrighted material in this book.

Every reasonable effort has been made to trace the owners of copyrighted material and to make due acknowledgment. Any errors or omissions drawn to our attention will be gladly rectified in future editions.

"Firefighter who lost nine fingers to frostbite successfully scales Europe's highest mountain" (excerpt) by Yumimi Pang. From the *Vancouver Sun*, August 17, 2006. Material reprinted with the express permission of "Pacific Newspaper Group Inc.," a CanWest Partnership.

"On Top of the World" (an excerpt from "Long Beach Teen is On Top of the World") by Nancy Wride. From the *Los Angeles Times*, May 21, 2007. Reprinted with permission.

Cover: Aerial view of Mount McKinley summit and the Alaskan Range–© Blaine Harrington III/Corbis/42-17305127

**Library and Archives Canada Cataloguing in Publication**

Samuel, Nigel
    The 10 mightiest mountains / Nigel Samuel.

Includes index.
ISBN 978-1-55448-509-3

    1. Readers (Elementary). 2. Readers—Mountains.
I. Title. II. Title: Ten mightiest mountains.

PE1117.S263 2007a          428.6          C2007-906703-4

1 2 3 4 5 6 7 8 9 10          10          17 16 15 14 13 12 11 10 09 08

Printed in Singapore

# Contents

6

18

34

# HIGH AND MIGHTY

**McKinley**
**20,320 feet**

**Mauna Kea**
**13,796 feet**

**Logan**
**19,551 feet**

**Aconcagua**
**22,835 feet**

When people meet celebrities, they are often surprised by how much smaller they look in real life compared to how they appear on the big screen. The opposite is true with mountains. For example, try to imagine the Sears Tower, which is 1,450 feet tall. Now check out Mount McKinley on the cover of this book. This mountain is taller than about 14 Sears Towers stacked on top of each other. Imagine how small you would feel standing at the base of the mountain!

Through the years, adventure seekers around the globe have been obsessed with conquering the planet's highest mountains. These climbers definitely have some dangerous work cut out for them. Mountains are found on every continent in the world and they make up 20 percent of the Earth's land surface. These magnificent landforms were created by incredibly strong forces of the moving plates just under the Earth's crust. Each peak is unique and each is always changing.

plates: *sections of the Earth's crust*

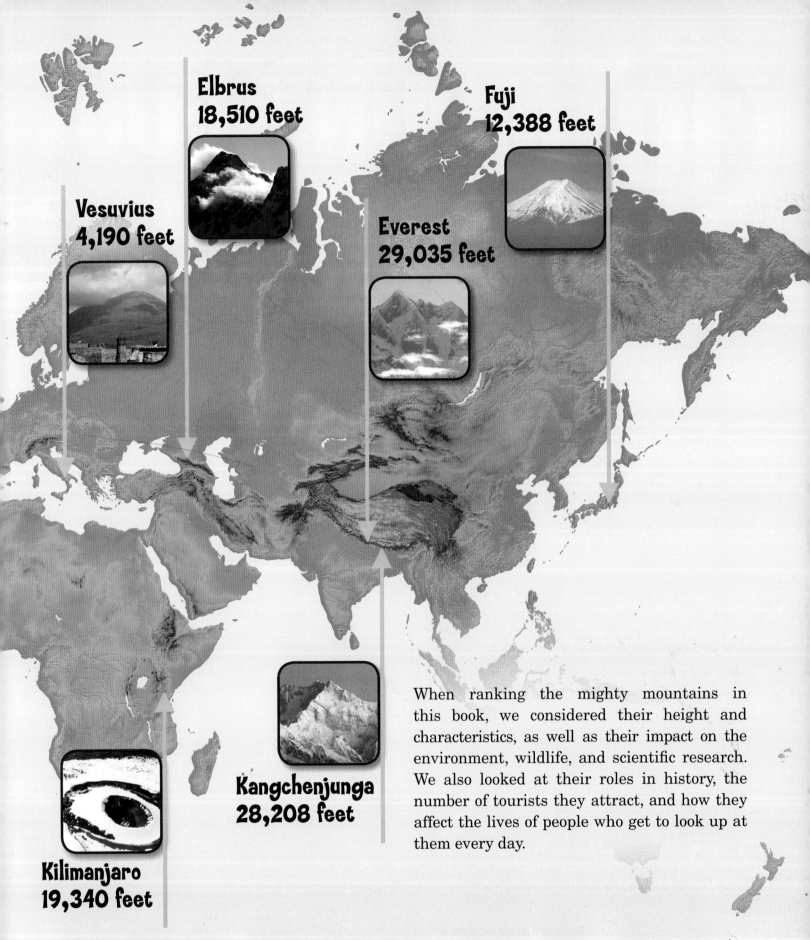

**Elbrus**
**18,510 feet**

**Fuji**
**12,388 feet**

**Vesuvius**
**4,190 feet**

**Everest**
**29,035 feet**

**Kangchenjunga**
**28,208 feet**

**Kilimanjaro**
**19,340 feet**

When ranking the mighty mountains in this book, we considered their height and characteristics, as well as their impact on the environment, wildlife, and scientific research. We also looked at their roles in history, the number of tourists they attract, and how they affect the lives of people who get to look up at them every day.

# WHICH MOUNTAIN IS THE MIGHTIEST OF THEM ALL?

# (10) MOUNT FUJI

*Mount Fuji is 70 miles away from Tokyo, Japan.*

**LOCATION: Honshu Island, Japan**

**HEIGHT: 12,388 feet**

**WOW FACTOR: It is the highest and most sacred mountain in Japan. It is also the world's most climbed mountain.**

Mount Fuji is a cone-shaped mountain with a snow-capped peak. It is the most distinctive landmark on Honshu Island and is a well-known symbol of Japan.

The color of Mount Fuji changes with the seasons. In winter, the mountain is covered with pure white snow. In summer, it looks almost blue, with a white cap of light snow and green forests on its lower slopes.

Each year, Mount Fuji attracts hundreds of thousands of tourists and local visitors. The Japanese consider the mountain sacred. It is their tradition to climb it at least once in their lifetime.

During most of the year, Mount Fuji's conditions can be quite dangerous due to strong winds, ice, snow, and avalanches. It is best to go during the official climbing season in July and August. At this time, the biggest challenge will be waiting in the long lines to get to the top! Maybe that's why the Japanese have a saying, "You are wise to climb Fuji once and a fool to climb it twice."

 Climbing Mount Fuji is a tradition among the Japanese. Think of one tradition that is observed by your family. What makes it special?

# MOUNT FUJI

The artist Katsushika Hokusai was obsessed with Mount Fuji because its peak is said to hold the secret to eternal life. This print is from his famous series 36 Views of Mount Fuji.

## THE LEGEND

At one time, many people believed Mount Fuji was haunted by trolls, goblins, and ghosts. Others believed that Mount Fuji was the home of a beautiful goddess. According to this legend, whenever the goddess saw a woman who looked better than herself, she became angry and burst into flames. For this reason, women weren't allowed to climb Fuji until the late 19th century.

## BEGINNINGS

Mount Fuji is a type of volcanic mountain known as a stratovolcano. It was created by a series of volcanic eruptions that happened during the past 10,000 years. The eruptions produced thick lava that did not flow easily. This lava cooled and hardened quickly before it could spread very far from the volcano's opening. This is what gives Mount Fuji its tall, steep cone shape.

---

stratovolcano: *tall volcano made up of alternating layers, or strata, of hardened lava and volcanic ash*

## STANDING TALL

Mount Fuji is located in the Fuji-Hakone-Izu National Park, which is only about 70 miles away from Japan's largest city, Tokyo. The mountain is a spectacular sight on land or from the sky. Air travelers can see the mountain as they fly over Honshu Island.

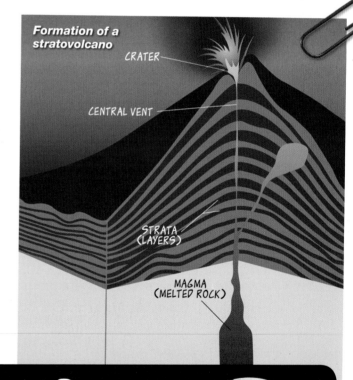

Formation of a stratovolcano

CRATER

CENTRAL VENT

STRATA (LAYERS)

MAGMA (MELTED ROCK)

## Quick Fact

It can take anywhere from three to seven hours to climb Mount Fuji and from two to five hours to get down. Climbing can be treacherous on windy days.

## The Expert Says...

"Aspire to be like Mount Fuji ... With your mind as high as Mount Fuji you can see all things clearly. And you can see all the forces that shape events; not just the things happening near to you."

— Miyamoto Musashi, Japanese martial arts master (1584–1645)

# GODZILLA'S BATTLEGROUND

**What does Mount Fuji have to do with Godzilla, a fictional Japanese movie character? Find out in this article.**

Every year hundreds of thousands of people visit Mount Fuji. This mighty mountain can be seen on postcards, on posters, and even in works of art in the finest Japanese museums. Some of the greatest authors have written about Mount Fuji. It has also starred in several Japanese movies.

Godzilla may be a fictional movie character but he is also a famous Japanese symbol. This giant prehistoric monster first appeared in 1954. Since then, he has been featured in 28 movies and is recognized all over the world. So it makes sense that the two should be featured together — in movies!

Mount Fuji has been used as a battleground in many Godzilla movies. During scenes when Godzilla is fighting another gruesome monster, Mount Fuji is always shown in the background. But in one famous scene in the movie *Godzilla vs. the Smog Monster*, the two creatures face off on top of the mountain. Smog Monster is a creature of pollution that humans have created. He can destroy anything, people included, just by flying over them. In the final scene, Godzilla kills the Smog Monster with an electric current. Godzilla overcomes the awesome Smog Monster on top of Mount Fuji!

GODZILLA–HULTON ARCHIVES/GETTY IMAGES; ALL OTHER IMAGES–SHUTTERSTOCK; MIYAMOTO MUSASHI–PUBLIC DOMAIN

## Quick Fact

Mount Fuji's last eruption, in 1708, was devastating. With millions living near the mountain today, the damage and death toll of an eruption would be unthinkable.

 Why do you think people would choose to live near a volcanic mountain, knowing that it could possibly erupt?

## Take Note

Mount Fuji comes in at #10 on our list. For people around the world, Mount Fuji is a symbol of Japan. What it lacks in height, it more than makes up for in beauty.
• Why do you think Mount Fuji was so inspiring to artists, writers, and filmmakers? Explain your answer.

# (9) MAUNA KEA

The world's largest astronomical lab is located on this Hawaiian mountain.

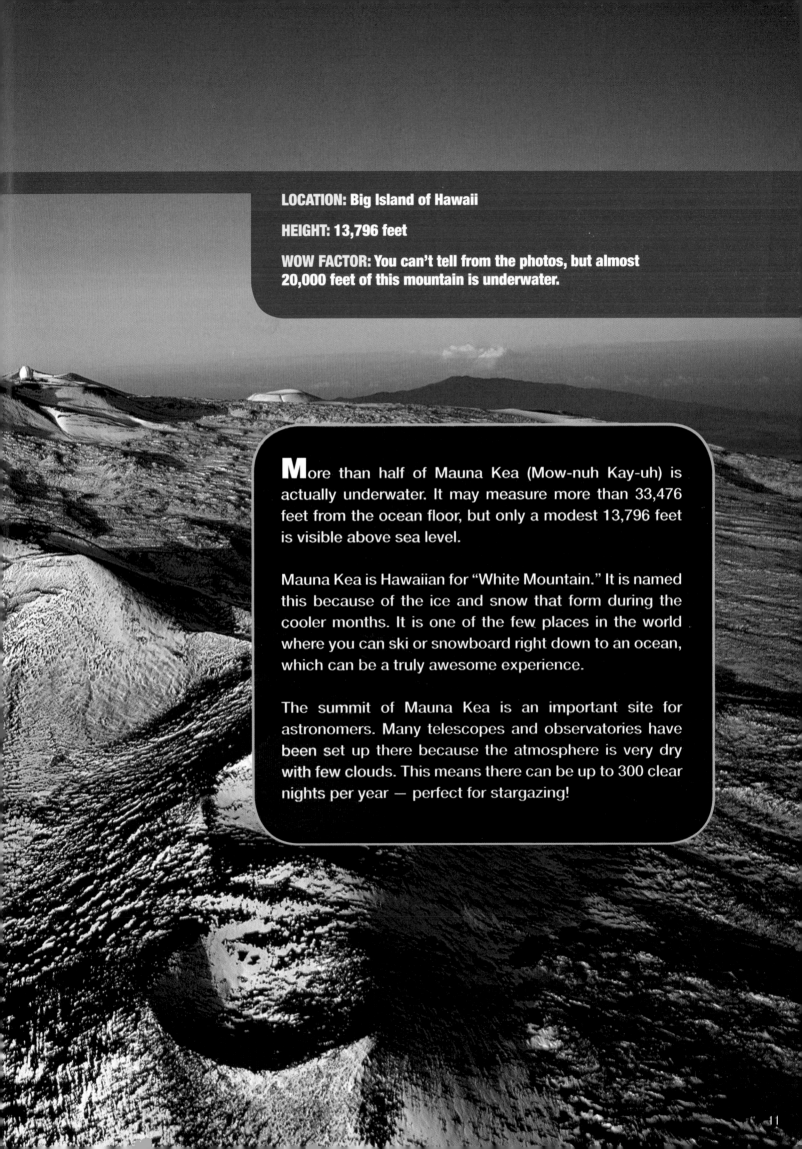

**LOCATION:** Big Island of Hawaii

**HEIGHT:** 13,796 feet

**WOW FACTOR:** You can't tell from the photos, but almost 20,000 feet of this mountain is underwater.

**M**ore than half of Mauna Kea (Mow-nuh Kay-uh) is actually underwater. It may measure more than 33,476 feet from the ocean floor, but only a modest 13,796 feet is visible above sea level.

Mauna Kea is Hawaiian for "White Mountain." It is named this because of the ice and snow that form during the cooler months. It is one of the few places in the world where you can ski or snowboard right down to an ocean, which can be a truly awesome experience.

The summit of Mauna Kea is an important site for astronomers. Many telescopes and observatories have been set up there because the atmosphere is very dry with few clouds. This means there can be up to 300 clear nights per year — perfect for stargazing!

## THE LEGEND

According to a Hawaiian legend, Mauna Kea's snow goddess never got along with the goddess of fire who lived in Mauna Loa, a nearby mountain. When the fire goddess threw fire at Mauna Kea, its snow goddess would smother the flames with her white cloak of snow. This explained why Mauna Loa erupted frequently while Mauna Kea stayed dormant and occasionally snow-covered. Being dormant, Mauna Kea is not currently active, but it is capable of erupting. It is quite unlike an extinct volcano. An extinct volcano is one that has not erupted for thousands of years and is not capable of erupting again.

## BEGINNINGS

Mauna Kea is a volcanic mountain known as a shield volcano. It was created over thousands of years by a buildup of hardened basaltic lava. Because this type of lava flows quickly and easily, it spreads very thinly. Sometimes it can even travel more than 12 miles from the volcano's opening! This is why shield volcanoes have a gently curved, shield-like appearance.

dormant: *sleeping; not erupting*
basaltic: *relating to a type of fine-grained volcanic rock*

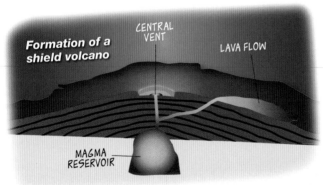

**Formation of a shield volcano**

CENTRAL VENT

LAVA FLOW

MAGMA RESERVOIR

## STANDING TALL

Mauna Kea's slopes are gentle and covered with lush green rain forests, as well as lands suitable for grazing animals and planting crops. During the winter time, the summit is covered in snow and ice. Sometimes lava flows out of the mountain and builds up. This makes the mountain taller every year.

N

Kohala

Mauna Kea

W

Hualalai

E

Mauna Loa

Kilauea

S

## The Expert Says...

"Mauna Kea's peaceful appearance is misleading. The volcano is not dead. It erupted many times between 60,000 and 4,000 years ago, and some periods of quiet during that time apparently lasted longer than 4,000 years. Given that record, future eruptions seem almost certain."

— Scientists at the Hawaiian Volcano Observatory

Compare Mauna Kea with Mount Fuji. How did each volcano get its shape?

# Seeing STARS

You don't need to go to Hollywood to see stars. After reading this article, you will see that a trip to Mauna Kea can also leave you starstruck!

Mauna Kea is home to many of the world's most powerful telescopes. It is truly a special place to study the stars and the universe. The summit offers unobstructed views. The skies are exceptionally clear most of the time, and there are no weather disturbances. In addition, Mauna Kea has gentle slopes, which makes it easy to build roads for transporting materials and equipment for building telescopes.

The famous twin Keck telescopes are found on Mauna Kea. They are optical telescopes and are also able to collect and focus infrared (heat) waves radiating from distant stars and galaxies. These telescopes are over 72 feet tall. They are the largest of their kind found anywhere in the world.

Astronomers using the giant Keck telescopes have made incredible discoveries. For instance, in 2004, a new planet was discovered. This was the largest transiting planet that passed between the Earth and a distant star outside our solar system.

The sunset is spectacular from the summit. Visitors can get an amazing view of the moon. They can also see Saturn and Jupiter through the telescopes.

unobstructed: clear view; not covered by something
optical telescopes: devices that gather and focus light to give a magnified view of a distant object

**?** Astronomers use the telescopes on Mauna Kea to study the universe. If you could use one of these telescopes, what objects in outer space would you most want to study? Explain.

## Quick Fact

A weird insect called the wekiu bug lives on top of Mauna Kea. It has a type of "anti-freeze" in its body so it can live on the ice found at the summit. It feeds on the fluids of other insects that die from the cold.

## Take Note

Mauna Kea stands tall at #9 on our list. It is an important center for astronomical discoveries and has a great impact on scientific research that will provide more information about our solar system and the universe.
• Which would you prefer to visit, Mount Fuji or Mauna Kea? Explain your reasons.

5    4    3    2    1

*Brrr! When the wind is strong, the temperature at Mount Elbrus can get as low as -58°F.*

# RUS

**LOCATION: The western Caucasus Mountains in Russia**

**HEIGHT: 18,510 feet**

**WOW FACTOR: Two heads are better than one! This is especially true in the case of the twin peaks of Mount Elbrus — Europe's highest mountain.**

Who needs border guards when you have a mountain range protecting your country? Mountain ranges often mark borders between countries. Invaders usually have to be pretty determined to make their way around a chain of mountains over 600 miles long! Throughout the years, the Caucasus mountain range has provided some great protection. This was especially true during World War II when these mountains made it really difficult for German troops to invade Russia.

Although the Caucasus mountain range consists of several mountains rising well above 16,000 feet, its crown jewel is Mount Elbrus. This twin-headed volcano is located in one of the most beautiful places in Russia. It is surrounded by glaciers, rivers, and mountain passes.

The landscape is rugged, but Mount Elbrus is home to many interesting plants and animals, including the brown bear. This bear is of the same species as the grizzly bear of North America. It is the national animal symbol of Russia and was the mascot of the 1980 Moscow Olympics.

Mount Elbrus has always been a challenge for mountain climbers because of its strong winds and cold weather. The first person to climb Mount Elbrus was a Russian mountaineer in 1829. Today, Mount Elbrus attracts skiers, hikers, and mountain climbers from all over the world.

# MOUNT ELBRUS

### THE LEGEND

In Greek mythology, the Greek god Zeus chained the titan Prometheus to a rock on Mount Elbrus. Prometheus was being punished for stealing the fire of the mountain and giving it to humans.

### BEGINNINGS

Mount Elbrus is a stratovolcano, like Mount Fuji at #10 on our list. Geologists believe that it rose from the ground about 10 million years ago. It was built up by layers of lava from countless eruptions over the years. The last volcanic eruption took place about 2,000 years ago. Today, Mount Elbrus is considered an extinct volcano. It is no longer capable of erupting at any time.

*titan: any child of the Earth and the sky whose family ruled until they were overthrown by Zeus*

The twin cones of Mount Elbrus are covered in a huge sheet of ice that is more than 1,250 feet thick in some areas.

## The Expert Says...

" She's our sacred mountain. Everything we have comes from her — our life, the water for our fields, for our flocks. The ice has been here for thousands of years. And so have we. "

— Iskhak Tilov, Mount Elbrus skiing guide and mountain climbing expert

### STANDING TALL

The mountain stands like a watchtower over the Caucasus mountain range, which was a natural barrier against invading armies throughout its history. Today, the mountain is better known for its beauty. Valleys are covered with beautiful flowers in the spring and summer. Glaciers from the Caucasus mountain range provide water for millions of people who live in the surrounding areas. Glacial erosion has created a scenic landscape of jagged ridges and exposed rock faces.

*glacial erosion: wearing away of land by glaciers*

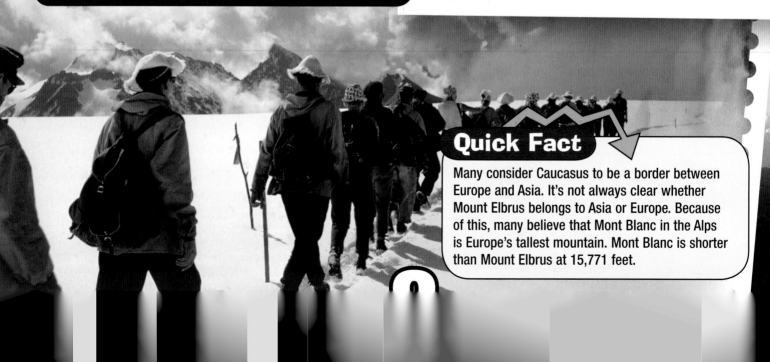

## Quick Fact

Many consider Caucasus to be a border between Europe and Asia. It's not always clear whether Mount Elbrus belongs to Asia or Europe. Because of this, many believe that Mont Blanc in the Alps is Europe's tallest mountain. Mont Blanc is shorter than Mount Elbrus at 15,771 feet.

# Firefighter who lost nine fingers to frostbite successfully scales Europe's highest mountain

A newspaper article from *The Vancouver Sun*, August 17, 2006
By YUMIMI PANG

**NORTH VANCOUVER** — Losing nine fingers on a climb last year was not enough to stop North Vancouver firefighter Erik Bjarnason from successfully scaling Europe's highest peak, Mount Elbrus, recently.

"I wanted to make sure I could still do it," said Bjarnason, 42, of his first climb since he made an attempt to scale Yukon's Mount Logan [in Canada].

In May 2005, Bjarnason, along with North Shore residents and North Shore rescue teammates … spent 72 hours trapped on Mount Logan during a storm where winds topped 62 mph and the mercury dipped to -22°F. They survived by huddling in an ice cave.

Bjarnason, whose gloves had blown away along with the group's tent, later had nine of his fingers amputated and spent six months in [the] hospital. …

---

amputated: *cut off by surgery*

When Bjarnason heard North Shore Rescue members were arranging a climb to Mount Elbrus, he couldn't resist. …

Bjarnason and four fellow North Shore Rescue members left Canada on July 12. They started in the Czech Republic with a few climbs and then moved on to Russia, where the 18,510-foot Mount Elbrus awaited, and they made it to the summit.

Bjarnason said that the trip was a complete success and is already planning to scale South America's highest point, Aconcagua, next year. He plans to take some people up in adapted wheelchairs on the next trip, just like he did several years ago to Mount Kilimanjaro.

**?** Do you think the feelings of accomplishment after a successful climb outweigh the risks of mountain climbing? Explain your answer.

Mount Elbrus's volcanic cone is under an ice cap that covers about 54 square miles.

## Take Note

Mount Elbrus is #8 on our list. It has an impact on the daily lives of the people living in its surroundings. The mountain is located in a range that provides water to its locals. Also, the mountain and its range played a vital role in history, especially during WWII.
- Compare Mount Elbrus with Mount Fuji or Mauna Kea. What are their similarities and differences?

# 7 MOUNT VES

*It may look pretty, but Mount Vesuvius has a very deadly past. It is still considered one of the world's most dangerous volcanoes.*

# UVIUS

LOCATION: Near the Bay of Naples, Italy

HEIGHT: 4,190 feet

WOW FACTOR: This deadly mountain caused the most famous volcanic eruption in history.

Mount Vesuvius is not a tall mountain, but it sure can make a lot of noise. It has a long history of devastating eruptions. The most famous eruption took place in A.D. 79, when Vesuvius buried the cities of Pompeii (Pom-pey) and Herculaneum (Hur-kyuh-ley-nee-uhm) under a blanket of extremely hot ashes and lava. Thousands of people died instantly.

The extent of the destruction can still be seen today because archeologists have uncovered the buried cities. People, animals, and buildings were encased in almost 66 feet of ashes. Many were scorched to death by the heat of the eruption. The volcanic ash covered the victims and set like cement. The ash had hardened around the bodies, but over time the bodies decayed, leaving an empty mold. Archeologists filled these molds with plaster and were able to see the expressions of fear and horror on the victims' faces.

Today, more than three million people live within 12 miles of the mountain. Vesuvius is still considered active and dangerous. If it erupts again, there could be another major disaster.

# MOUNT VESUVIUS

## THE LEGEND

One Greek legend claims that a giant named Mimas was imprisoned in Mount Vesuvius by the god of fire and metal. Mimas caused earthquakes and volcanic eruptions each time he struggled to free himself. The Greeks and Romans also regarded Mount Vesuvius as the home of their hero Hercules. The town of Herculaneum, built at its base, was named after him.

### Quick Fact

Excavations in the city of Pompeii uncovered hundreds of objects that were preserved very well by the volcanic ash. Jewelry, gold coins, artwork, and household objects have given us revealing details about everyday life in ancient Rome.

excavations: *acts of digging to explore a buried site*

**The ruins of the city of Pompeii sit in the shadow of Mount Vesuvius.**

## BEGINNINGS

Vesuvius is a stratovolcano. Its eruption, in A.D. 79, was named a *Plinian* eruption after the ancient philosopher Pliny. Pliny was the first person to write about this type of eruption. Plinian eruptions usually create huge pine-tree-shaped clouds above the volcano's crater. During these eruptions, poisonous gases, ash, and little stones are thrown from the volcano.

## STANDING TALL

Vesuvius stands in a heavily populated part of southern Italy. The volcano is active, and sometimes it still emits smoke. Mount Vesuvius and the cities of Pompeii and Herculaneum are important reminders of the overwhelming power of nature.

crater: *bowl-shaped hole at the top of a volcano; formed when Plinian eruptions blast off the peaks*

**?** If you were the mayor of nearby Naples, what plan would you put in place to protect the people in case of an eruption?

## The Expert Says...

"A Royal Observatory was established on the slopes of the mountain in 1844. Since that time, scientists have kept a constant watch over the volcano during and between eruptions."

— David I. Kertzer, Ph.D., Provost and Paul Dupee University Professor of Social Science, Brown University

**The volcanic ash hardened around Vesuvius's victims, capturing their final moments in great detail.**

# I Was There ...

Pliny the Younger was a lawyer, author, and philosopher in ancient Rome. He was there when Vesuvius erupted in A.D. 79. This letter was written by Pliny while Vesuvius was erupting. It is the earliest document of a volcanic eruption in history.

On a rising scale of 1 to 8, Vesuvius has an eruption intensity of 5. This can create an ash cloud as high as 15 miles. It can throw out over 300,000 cubic miles of lava and ashes.

He [my uncle, also named Pliny] was at Miseneum in his capacity as commander of the fleet on the 24th of August [A.D. 79], when between 2 and 3 in the afternoon my mother drew his attention to a cloud of unusual size and appearance. ... The cloud was rising from a mountain ... it was Vesuvius. I can best describe its shape by likening it to a pine tree. It rose into the sky on a very long "trunk" from which spread some "branches." I imagine it had been raised by a sudden blast, which then weakened, leaving the cloud unsupported so that its own weight caused it to spread sideways. Some of the cloud was white, in other parts there were dark patches of dirt and ash. The sight of it made the scientist in my uncle determined to see it from closer at hand.

He ordered a boat made ready. He offered me the opportunity of going along, but I preferred to study ... Ash was falling onto the ships now, darker and denser the closer they went. Now it was bits of pumice, and rocks that were blackened and burned and shattered by the fire. Now the sea is shoal; debris from the mountain blocks the shore. He paused for a moment wondering whether to turn back as the helmsman urged him. "Fortune helps the brave," he said. "Head for Pomponianus."

pumice: volcanic rock full of holes from trapped air bubbles
shoal: shallow

## Quick Fact

Pliny the Younger's uncle was known as Pliny the Elder. Pliny the Elder tried to rescue people who were close to the mountain. Unfortunately, he died when he was overcome by the fumes of the eruption.

## Take Note

Vesuvius is not a tall mountain. But its eruption in A.D. 79 buried cities and captured a moment in history some 2,000 years ago. This mountain makes its way to the #7 spot because it is an enduring reminder of the awesome power of nature.
• Find out more about archeologists' discoveries at Pompeii. What can you learn about life in early Rome?

*Mount Logan is North America's second-tallest peak.*

AN

**LOCATION:** Yukon, Canada

**HEIGHT:** 19,551 feet

**WOW FACTOR:** Its base covers an area of over 500 square miles, which is larger than that of any other mountain in the world.

You will find Mount Logan standing majestically in what is known as "the mountain kingdom of North America."

Mount Logan isn't just tall, it's also massive. It is believed to have the largest base circumference of all the mountains in the world. It is a part of the St. Elias mountain range in the Yukon Territory, which is located in northwest Canada. Aside from the North and South Poles, this mountain range has the largest ice fields in the world. In fact, Mount Logan is even taller than it appears, because it actually starts several thousand feet below these ice fields.

All rock and ice, the peak of Mount Logan has the reputation of being too cold to support human or animal life. The mountain is quite hard to get to because there are no roads or tracks leading to its peak. The only way to get to the top is either by helicopter or by a grueling two-week trek. Only the most daring and determined climbers reach the top, and few stay long enough to truly admire the pristine beauty of glaciers, jagged ridges, and steep rock faces.

circumference: *distance around a circle*

# MOUNT LOGAN

## THE LEGEND

Aboriginal people, who have lived in the region for generations, view the harsh and forbidding environment of Mount Logan as a part of nature to be respected. Some tribes believe that spirits live in the mountain and appear in the form of snow or frost.

## BEGINNINGS

Mount Logan was formed millions of years ago when the North American continent pushed against the Pacific land mass. The boundary where they met buckled, creating the St. Elias mountain range. The land masses are still pushing against each other, so Mount Logan is still rising very slowly.

forbidding: *uninviting; making progress difficult*

## STANDING TALL

Glaciers carve the surface of Mount Logan, giving it a rugged and unique look. The mountain holds 300 miles of continuous ice fields, which makes this the largest ice cap outside of Antarctica and Greenland. The mountain is largely composed of granodiorite, which is a type of plutonic rock.

plutonic: *formed when magma is solidified below the surface of the Earth*

### Quick Fact

A temperature of -106.6°F was recorded in 1991 on Mount Logan. It was the lowest temperature outside of Anarctica. Up to three feet of snow can fall in a single storm.

With such cold and sometimes extreme weather conditions, why would people still want to climb Mount Logan?

## The Expert Says...

"Mount Logan is big, remote, and beautiful beyond words. ... It remains a real and pristine climbing adventure."

— George Dunn, a certified alpine guide

In 2001, a team of scientists and mountaineers lived in these tents for four-and-a-half weeks while they studied the ice on Mount Logan.

# SECRETS IN THE ICE

Why are scientists so interested in studying the ice on Mount Logan? You might be surprised by the answers in these fact cards!

## Climate Change

Mount Logan is home to some of the most extensive glaciers and ice fields in the world. Because the temperature in the area remains below the freezing point all year, the ice never melts! Instead, the snow that falls, collects and becomes layers of ice over the years. The layers of ice can indicate when each layer was formed and how cold it was at the time. In some places, the ice layers can be almost a thousand feet thick. Way down where the ice touches the mountain, it may be thousands of years old.

Scientists study the ice layers in the ice cores from Mount Logan. This helps scientists understand past climates and predict future climate trends in the Pacific region.

cores: *columns of ice, soil, and rock removed with a hollow drill*

## Pollution

The study of ice cores can also tell scientists something about the level of air pollution. Small amounts of dust and pollutants in the air get trapped in the snow that falls on Mount Logan. This snow turns into ice with the pollutants trapped inside. By studying the ice cores, scientists can determine the changes in pollution levels over time.

## Quick Fact

The glaciated plateau on Mount Logan is about 12 miles long and three miles wide.

## Take Note

Mount Logan offers scientists and researchers an opportunity to gather ice cores to study climatic changes and air pollution. For playing an important role in advancing our knowledge about our world's past and future, Mount Logan ranks #6 on our list.
• Compare Mount Logan with another mountain that you have read about so far.

*Mount McKinley is one of the world's coldest peaks. Need proof? Wind speeds of almost 100 mph and temperatures that feel like -94°F make the summit's climate colder than the North Pole.*

# INLEY

**LOCATION:** Alaska, U.S.A.

**HEIGHT:** 20,320 feet

**WOW FACTOR:** It's the tallest mountain in North America.

Imagine a mountain that's taller than about 14 Sears Towers stacked together! Mount McKinley is a natural wonder. It is found in the state of Alaska, and is part of the 600-mile-long Alaskan mountain range. Mount McKinley rises majestically into the northern sky and is known for its beautiful sunsets. It is home to grizzly bears, big horn sheep, elk, marmots, and golden eagles.

This mountain is too high, too windy, and much too cold for humans. It is not a friendly place for mountain climbers because of avalanches and powerful earthquakes. The second-strongest earthquake ever recorded occurred nearby in 1964.

This mountain is also known by the name *Denali*, which means "the high one" in the language of the Aboriginal people who live in the area. They believe that Denali belongs to nature and should be left untouched and unspoiled. In 1897, the mountain was renamed after President William McKinley.

 Do you think Denali is a better name than Mount McKinley? Why?

# MOUNT McKINLEY

## THE LEGEND

According to legend, the native people living near the mountain believed it was created to protect their ancestors. They treated the mountain with respect, and they avoided gazing at its summit.

## BEGINNINGS

Like Mount Logan, this mountain was formed millions of years ago when two plates pressed against each other. The pressure buckled the plates and created a mountain when one plate was pushed down while the other got pushed up. Other mountains along most of North America's west coast were also formed this way.

## STANDING TALL

Rated by sheer bulk, or mass, Mount McKinley is bigger than Mount Everest, which is the highest mountain in the world. The rocks at the base of Mount McKinley are composed of granite and slate, and they are covered by very hard ice, hundreds of feet thick. McKinley is located in the heart of the Denali National Park and Preserve. Its six-million acres are filled with lakes, caves, forests, 39 species of mammals, and 167 species of birds.

### Quick Fact

This mountain's climate is so harsh that only half of the climbers actually reach the summit. Every year, around a dozen climbers have to be rescued, which costs taxpayers around $400,000.

**?** Do you think that taxpayers should have to pay for this? What solutions would you suggest to solve this problem?

*Watch out! Piles of garbage are a common sight along McKinley trails. Because it's too cold for the garbage to rot, it lasts forever unless it's removed.*

### The Expert Says...

"It's just so beautiful. It has everything other mountains have, only on a much bigger scale. It has bigger crevasses, fiercer weather, steeper slopes, even more sunlight.

— Mike Haugen, teacher and mountain guide

crevasses: *deep cracks in sheets of ice*

# BLAZING the Trail

## An article about Barbara Washburn

You might be surprised to discover that only about 10 percent of the mountaineers who climb McKinley are women. This number might be even lower if it weren't for a trailblazer named Barbara Washburn. In 1947, this college professor joined her husband on an expedition and became the first woman to ever climb Mount McKinley. She shares her experience in these quotes.

Washburn went on to make many other historic climbs while still holding her place as teacher, explorer, cartographer, and mother. What a woman!

cartographer: *mapmaker*

> It was like looking out the windows of heaven ... It was truly the way I had imagined heaven to be when I was a child.

> Before me lay 100,000 square miles of Alaska. Snow-covered mountains and terrain stretched to the horizon in a view that left me breathless.

> The wind was gusting to 30 miles an hour and the temperature was 25 degrees below zero.

## Quick Fact

In 1970, Arlene Blum led the first all-female climbing team to the top of McKinley. When she first tried to join an expedition, she was told she could stay at base camp and do the cooking. Blum says, "When I was told no, I became like a compressed spring — the harder I was pushed down, the more forcefully I pushed back." Blum is also a scientist who has made several important discoveries in biochemistry.

On top of the world! Barbara Washburn (right) and her husband Bradford at the peak of Mount McKinley

## Take Note

Mount McKinley stands at #5 on our list. It is the tallest mountain in North America. Also, it has an impact on the lives of mountain climbers. The summit intrigues and challenges even the most experienced mountain climbers.
• What does it take to be a mountain climber? Do some research and list special personal attributes needed, as well as the type of training involved, to prepare for a trip to Mount McKinley.

*Each year, an estimated 20,000 people attempt to reach the top of Mount Kilimanjaro.*

# ...ANJARO

**LOCATION:** Tanzania, Africa

**HEIGHT:** 19,340 feet

**WOW FACTOR:** It is the tallest mountain in Africa, and it's taller than any other mountain that's not part of a range.

Mount Kilimanjaro rises majestically in a relatively flat landscape of open grasslands, lakes, and lush tropical forests. Its snowcapped peak is clear and bright and visible from a great distance. From any direction, this freestanding mountain is an unforgettable sight. It is Africa's pride and the continent's most famous landmark.

The weather is hard to resist. It attracts tourists and regular mountain climbers from all over the world. It's not freezing cold like Mount Logan or Mount McKinley. The average temperature at the base is 77°F to 86°F. Average temperatures at the peak range from 14°F to -4°F.

Mount Kilimanjaro is more than a tourist attraction. The lower slopes are used for crops. The climate is perfect for growing world-class coffee.

MOUNT KILIMANJARO—CORBIS

31

# MOUNT KILIMANJARO

## THE LEGEND

No one knows how the mountain got its name, but it has been legendary since ancient times. Ptolemy, a great Greek astronomer in the second century, wrote of a "great snow mountain" in a mysterious land. To the locals, the mountain was believed to be home to spirits.

Tourists in Africa love to get a glimpse of Mount Kilimanjaro.

## BEGINNINGS

Mount Kilimanjaro is a dormant stratovolcano, made up of layers of ash and lava. This mighty mountain was formed 750,000 years ago. Three separate peaks came together as a result of volcanic eruptions. At one time, Mount Kilimanjaro was much higher than it is today. It has been gradually worn away by erosion.

## STANDING TALL

Mount Kilimanjaro is shaped like a cone and crowned with a snowcapped peak. The government of Tanzania created Mount Kilimanjaro National Park to protect the area. Today, this mighty mountain is not shining as brightly because there is less snow on its peak. According to scientists, almost 80 percent of Kilimanjaro's ice cap has disappeared between 1912 and 2000! Scientists say that global warming may cause the snow on the top to completely disappear by the year 2020.

---

erosion: *gradual wearing away of the earth's surface by wind and water*

**?** This mountain is famous for its snowy peak, but the snow is rapidly disappearing due to global warming. What are other consequences of climate change?

## The Expert Says...

" As wide as all the world, great, high, and unbelievably white in the sun, was the square top of Mount Kilimanjaro. "

— Ernest Hemingway, American writer and winner of the Nobel Prize in Literature

## Quick Fact

African officials are very worried about the melting ice on the summit of Mount Kilimanjaro. They are afraid that tourism to their country will drop. This could severely affect the country's economy.

# From Base to Peak

This chart shows the five zones of Mount Kilimanjaro. Each has its own community of plant and animal life-forms, making the mountain unique.

## ICE-COVERED PEAK

The volcanic crater is covered by glaciers. These glaciers provide a large portion of the region's water supply.

 The melting glacier is already causing water shortages. What can be done to stop further damage?

## 13,000 TO 16,000 FEET

The temperature is always fluctuating in this alpine desert. Only lichens, mosses, and the occasional spider can survive.

## 9,000 TO 13,000 FEET

When mountain climbers reach this zone, they start to climb slowly due to the air's reduced oxygen. Only hardy species of plants thrive in cold and dry weather conditions on this highland desert. During the day, the sun is extremely intense. However, the nighttime is cool and clear.

## 6,000 TO 9,000 FEET

The rain forest on this zone is damp and drenched in rain. Animals, birds, and plants thrive here because of these conditions.

## Take Note

Mount Kilimanjaro secures the #4 spot on our list, ahead of Mount McKinley. It supports a variety of plant and animal life-forms. It also attracts many tourists to the country every year.

- Research and find out how Mount Kilimanjaro is important to the livelihood of the people living in the region.

## BASE OF MOUNTAIN

This is an agricultural zone with fertile soil. The climate is ideal for crops, especially coffee.

*Fossils of marine life found on the mountain are evidence that it was once part of the ocean floor.*

MOUNT KANGCHENJUNGA-©BRIAN A. VIKANDER/CORBIS/BV008371I

# CHENJUNGA

**LOCATION:** On the border of India and Nepal

**HEIGHT:** 28,208 feet

**WOW FACTOR:** It's India's highest mountain, and the third highest in the world.

Kangchenjunga (Kahn-chuhn-jung-guh) is a massive mountain with five impressive peaks. Three of them, including the main peak, are located in India. The other two peaks are in Nepal. Kangchenjunga was considered the world's highest mountain until 1953, when the title went to Mount Everest.

Kangchenjunga is famous for its natural beauty. On a clear day, it looks like a white wall hanging from the sky. Its lower slopes are marked by deep gorges, majestic oaks, and beautiful magnolia and sycamore trees. Plantations of tea add a sweet fragrance to the whole area.

Situated in a remote part of India, Kangchenjunga is home to some very rare wildlife. The red panda and the snow leopard live on the forested slopes of the mountain.

Mount Kangchenjunga was rarely visited by outsiders until recently, when the area was opened up to visitors. More hikers and climbers are now able to enjoy the beauty of this majestic mountain and to scale its peak.

 What are the different ways a mountain can help a local economy?

# MOUNT KANGCHENJUNGA

### THE LEGEND

To the people who live in the area, Kangchenjunga is sacred. Its name means "The Five Treasures of the Snow," which refers to Kangchenjunga's five peaks. The peaks represent treasures of gold, silver, gems, grain, and holy books. They are thought to be gifts from the heavens.

 **Why do you think so many mountains are considered sacred to the people living near them?**

### BEGINNINGS

Mount Kangchenjunga was formed by a geologic uplift. At one time, the Himalayan mountain range was a coastal area, and India was an island around 4,000 miles south of the Asian continent. About 140 million years ago, the island started drifting north. It crushed the softer coastal land. Kangchenjunga was one of the peaks on the ridges that formed as a result.

### STANDING TALL

Kangchenjunga is part of the Himalayan mountain range. On this mountain, heavy rainfalls and high levels of precipitation help to create monsoons. The mountain's melting ice provides water to the rivers, such as the Indus, Ganges, and Brahmaputra, that flow through India.

---

precipitation: *rain, snow, and hail falling in a given period*

### Quick Fact

On May 25, 1955, British mountaineers Joe Brown and George Bend became the first people to successfully climb Kangchenjunga. Ginette Harrison, in 1998, was the first and only woman to accomplish this feat.

## The Expert Says...

" … we can scarcely believe [Kangchenjunga] is part of the solid Earth on which we stand; and so high it seems part of the very sky itself. "

— Sir Francis Younghusband, author of *The Epic of Mount Everest*

*Water flows from Kangchenjunga into the Ganges River.*

**10**   **9**   **8**   **7**   **6**

# Win One for Nature

**Conservation scores a victory on Mount Kangchenjunga. Check out this article.**

The wildest places on our planet have always been a refuge for some of the rarest animals. Mount Kangchenjunga is one such place. It is the ideal home for one of the rarest and most beautiful big cats, the snow leopard.

*Don't worry — the snow leopard prefers to stay away from humans.*

The snow leopard is shy and often referred to as a "silent hunter." It does not roar like lions or tigers. It prefers to stay away from humans.

As the human population in Kangchenjunga increased, the snow leopard started to roam farther away from its Himalyan home base to live and hunt. It showed up in places all the way from China in the east to Uzbekistan in Central Asia. When it started to go after sheep and goats, local residents hunted it down. Poaching was another problem. Some people killed the animal for its beautiful fur. The animal was seriously endangered; the population of snow leopards dropped to as low as 1,000 in 1960.

However, digital and GPS (Global Positioning System) technology has allowed conservation groups to track the animal and keep it from going astray. Unlike many wild animals that do not reproduce in a protected environment, the snow leopard has no trouble breeding. Their numbers in Asia have since increased to between 6,000 and 10,000. That's still not enough for this animal to be taken off the endangered species list. But it is a victory!

## Take Note

At #3, Kangchenjunga has a reputation for its height and natural beauty. It is home to some rare and beautiful wildlife and plants. It attracts tourists and mountain climbers, and locals depend on it for their livelihood.

• There are very few people living in and around Kangchenjunga, yet the mountain affects the lives of millions. Why is that so?

# 2 MOUNT ACO

*The wind at Mount Aconcagua is known to its local residents as viento blanco, which means white wind.*

# NCAGUA

MOUNT ACONCAGUA–© S. P. GILLETTE/CORBIS/AX065003

**LOCATION:** Argentina, South America

**HEIGHT:** 22,835 feet

**WOW FACTOR:** It's the highest mountain in South America, and the highest outside of Asia.

**M**ount Aconcagua (Ah-kon-kah-gwah) is in the Andes, which is South America's longest chain of mountains. The Andes runs along the west coast of South America. It has numerous peaks as high as 16,000 feet, but Mount Aconcagua is the tallest, rising to a staggering 22,835 feet.

This mountain is very popular among climbers. It is technically an easy mountain, especially if climbers take the normal route from the north. There are no treacherous rock faces or ice walls. From the summit, climbers and hikers have an open view of the Andes, its glaciers, and its many ice-capped peaks. The mountain offers another treat for visitors — a chance to spot two of the world's largest birds, the purple eagle and the Andean condor.

To get to the top of Mount Aconcagua, climbers have to deal with the usual dangers of high altitude and extreme changes in weather. Each year, fewer than a third of the climbers make it to the summit. One reason is because the wind can blow at speeds close to 100 mph.

# MOUNT ACONCAGUA

### THE LEGEND

The name Aconcagua comes from the Inca language. It means "stone sentinel," which is a guard carved in stone. This suggests that the early native people respected the mountain.

### BEGINNINGS

Aconcagua is not a volcano, even though it is located in a region of volcanic activity. The mountain was formed millions of years ago when the Pacific tectonic ocean plate moved under the South American plate. This resulted in an uplifting of sedimentary rocks, which formed the Andes.

sedimentary: *rocks in strata formed from sediment*

N

Paraguay

Chile

Argentina

Brazil

○ **Aconcagua**

Uruguay

## Quick Fact

Mount Aconcagua is the second-tallest of the Seven Summits. The Seven Summits are the highest mountains on each of the world's seven continents. The other six mountains are: Kilimanjaro, Vinson Massif, Kosciuszko, Everest, Elbrus, and McKinley.

### STANDING TALL

This spectacular mountain has two peaks, which are joined by sharp, rocky ridges formed by glacial ice. The top is too cold to support wildlife, but the lower slopes are home to foxes, rabbits, and mountain lions. Birds of prey make their homes on the isolated rocky cliffs. Glaciers, rivers, and lakes add to the beauty of the landscape.

*You don't have to be an expert to climb Mount Aconcagua, but it helps! Climbers need to be careful because some routes are harder than others.*

? If you had to promote Mount Aconcagua, what would you say or do to attract more climbers to this mighty mountain?

## The Expert Says ...

" Of the seven continental summits, Aconcagua lies second only to Everest ... However, it is one of the world's highest and toughest treks. "

— Harry Kikstra, author of *Aconcagua: Summit of South America*

# MOUNTAIN CHAT

**Want to know more about Mount Aconcagua?**
**Check out these fascinating fact cards!**

## ALTITUDE SICKNESS

Mountain climbers often under-estimate the risk of altitude sickness, which can cause death. Near the top of the summit, the air is thin and it affects breathing. When climbers experience symptoms such as headaches, nausea, vomiting, dizziness, and insomnia, they should descend immediately. It is important to take in lots of fluid and to climb up slowly, so the body has time to adjust to the high altitude.

## THE GOOD OLD MULE

Some climbers travel with mules. A mule is a lot of help — it can carry as much as 130 pounds of food and supplies. In the past, mules were used to carry down garbage from campsite dumps. Today, climbers are responsible for keeping the mountain clean.

## A MUMMY

What a shocking discovery! In 1985, a mummy of a young boy was discovered on Mount Aconcagua. It was located on the southwest side of the mountain. According to archeologists, this mummy was over 450 years old.

## ENDANGERED SPECIES

The Andean condor, which makes its home in the wild and open space of Mount Aconcagua, is a national symbol of Argentina. This large bird of prey has a wingspan close to 10 feet — the largest of any bird in the world. Today, the condor is protected to save it from extinction. To increase its numbers, biologists incubate and hatch condor eggs. Once the chicks are old enough to survive on their own, they are released into the world.

## Take Note

Mount Aconcagua is a tourist attraction, having a positive impact on the livelihood of the people. And climbers place it high on the list of world summits to scale. For all these reasons, Mount Aconcagua easily takes the #2 spot on our list.

• Go online and read more about climbing Mount Aconcagua. If you were a guide, what advice would you give to climbers regarding clothing, food items, and mental and physical preparation?

5     4     3     **2**     1

# 1 MOUNT EVE

*Mount Everest is known as the ultimate challenge because it is physically demanding for even the most experienced climbers.*

# REST

**LOCATION:** Nepal, Tibet

**HEIGHT:** 29,035 feet

**WOW FACTOR:** The highest, most famous, and most awe-inspiring mountain on the planet!

MOUNT EVEREST—CORBIS

"**S**ir, I have discovered the highest mountain in the world!"

A mathematician at the Surveyor Office in India made a surprising discovery in 1852. He found out that Peak XV was taller than any mountain recorded at the time. Peak XV was renamed Mount Everest, after Colonel Sir George Everest. He was Surveyor General of India from 1830 to 1843.

Mount Everest is spectacular for its jagged peaks, glaciers, and emerald lakes. This king of the mountains gave worldwide fame to Edmund Hillary and Tenzing Norgay. They were the first to reach its summit in 1953. It was a feat then considered impossible. Today, with mountain guides, modern equipment, and a whole lot of nerve, many climbers scale Mount Everest each year.

Still, Everest is known for its dangers and treacherous conditions. Its Death Zone, an area near the summit, poses a serious threat to climbers because of the low level of oxygen, storms, and strong winds.

# MOUNT EVEREST

### THE LEGEND

Sherpas are people who live in the Himalayas and are known for their mountaineering skills. They believe that mountains are the sacred homes of gods. They call Mount Everest *Chomulungma*, which means "Goddess Mother of the Land."

### BEGINNINGS

Mount Everest was created by a collision of two continental plates. This natural wonder began to form 60 million years ago and has been slowly growing ever since. Today, Everest is still growing due to underground land movement. It is rising and shifting by half an inch each year. Earthquakes, landslides, and avalanches occur frequently due to the unstable conditions of the mountain range.

### STANDING TALL

The mountain range is wild and rugged, rising up from the surrounding foothills of Nepal and Tibet like a huge backbone made of stone. Wildlife, which includes the majestic golden eagle, abounds in this beautiful place. Mount Everest looks down upon the tops of other tall mountains, so the view is spectacular. Everywhere you look, you can see rows of snowcapped peaks and glaciers. These glaciers are an important source of fresh water for many of the people in the region, including people living in India and China.

## Quick Fact

The deadliest year in Mount Everest's climbing history was 1996, when 15 people died trying to reach the summit. As of 2006, 2,250 have scaled the Everest and about 200 climbers have died on the mountain.

**?** For mountain climbers, scaling Mount Everest is the ultimate challenge. What is one thing that you most want to do for adventure?

*Sir Edmund P. Hillary (left) and his guide Tenzing Norgay*

## The Expert Says...

Mount Everest is the pinnacle of the Earth's surface.

— Stephen James O'Meara, author of *Faces: People, Places, and Cultures*

pinnacle: *highest point*

10    9    8    7    6

# ON TOP OF THE WORLD

A newspaper article from the *Los Angeles Times*, May 21, 2007
By Nancy Wride

Samantha Larson during her Everest adventure

**"I** feel really incredible," Samantha Larson, 18, said ... describing her sense of accomplishment after having conquered Mount Everest — the tallest place on Earth.

It was about 9:30 AM Monday, Nepal time, and the Long Beach teenager was waiting below a base camp on the side of Mount Everest for a helicopter to take her trekking group, including her father, to Katmandu. ...

The Larsons also [became], perhaps, the first father-daughter team to conquer the so-called Seven Summits, the highest peaks on each of the seven continents.

They have climbed mountains as a team since Larson was a middle-school student lugging along algebra homework and a plastic oboe to stay in practice during the rigorous weeks involved in such ascents.

Describing the difficulty of the climb, Larson said the altitude drains all appetite; after gobbling down a chocolate bar, she subsisted for several days only on water to ward off dehydration. The temperature on the snowy peak reached "probably 30 below," she said.

"Your whole body is completely covered with [goose] down; your face is covered with your oxygen mask and goggles," she said.

Still, the conditions on the summit were daunting.

"On summit day, we wore everything," she said, referring to the garments they had packed to keep warm. ...

The party included climbers who had previously climbed mountains with her and her father. ...

rigorous: *demanding*
subsisted: *survived*
daunting: *overwhelming; frightening*

## Take Note

At #1 on our list, Mount Everest is the highest mountain on the planet — it seems to reach into the sky. Everest is the ultimate challenge for mountain climbers from all over the world. The mountain is also an important source of fresh water, and it is home to wildlife.

- Like many sports, mountain climbing is both a mental and physical challenge. If you had the chance to climb only one mountain, which one would it be? Explain your choice.

## We Thought ...

**Here are the criteria we used in ranking the 10 mightiest mountains.**

**The mountain:**
- Is an awe-inspiring natural landform
- Is a beautiful sight and the pride of the people
- Has the tallest, most imposing peak in its surroundings
- Attracts tourists and mountain climbers
- Is the home of rare plants and endangered species
- Affects the history and life of people living in its vicinity
- Provides a challenge for climbers and hikers

## What Do You Think?

1. Do you agree with our ranking? If you don't, try ranking them yourself. Justify your ranking with data from your own research and reasoning. You may refer to our criteria, or you may want to draw up your own list of criteria.

2. Here are three other mountains we considered but in the end did not include in our top 10 list: K2, Lhotse, and Vinson Massif.
   • Find out more about them. Do you think they should have made our list? Give reasons for your response.
   • Are there other mountains that you think should have made our list? Explain your choices.

# Index